ESSA

# HILAIRE
# BELLOC

British Library Cataloguing-in-Publication Data
A catalogue record for this book is available from the
British Library

# Hilaire Belloc

Hilaire Belloc was born in La Celle-Saint-Cloud, France in July of 1870. He was raised in England, and spent much of his boyhood in Slindon, West Sussex.

After being educated at John Henry Newman's Oratory School in Edgbaston, Birmingham, Belloc served his term of French military service with an artillery regiment near Toul. After his military service, in 1892, Belloc proceeded to Balliol College, Oxford, as a History scholar. He became President of the Oxford Union, the University's debating society, and began to establish his reputation as a brilliant but intemperate speaker.

Graduating from Oxford with First Class honours, Belloc was aggrieved not to be offered a fellowship, a failure he put down to his Catholicism. Belloc's faith was the guiding force of his life, and he believed it to be central to the survival of Western civilisation, famously declaring "the faith is Europe and Europe is the faith". After Oxford he became friends with G. K Chesterton and George Bernard Shaw and these three, together with H. G. Wells, came to be known as 'The Big Four' of Edwardian letters. In 1902, Belloc became a naturalised British citizen. That same year, he published his *The Path to Rome,* a now-iconic piece of travel writing which has remained in print for more than a century. Five years later, Belloc published his best-known work, *Cautionary Tales for Children* - a parody of the cautionary tales that were popular in the 19th century.

In 1906, Belloc went into politics, standing as a Liberal candidate in the 1906 General Election, winning the seat of South Salford. He stood as an independent at the next election in 1910, narrowing retaining his seat, but losing it when a second General Election was called later the same year. A one-time member of the Fabian Society, Belloc now moved decisively to the right, though he remained a political maverick, equally hostile to both unbridled capitalism and socialism.

His Parliamentary career over, Belloc took on a huge workload as a freelance writer, becoming editor of the political weekly *Eye Witness,* which had a circulation of over 100,000. During the First World War he edited *Land and Water,* a journal devoted to the progress of the war. His son, Louis, a member of the Royal Flying Corps, was killed in action. Postwar, Belloc continued to be one of the most prolific writers of his era, publishing his best known non-fiction works: *The Servile State* (1912), *Europe and Faith* (1920) and *The Jews* (1922). In 1942, he suffered a debilitating stroke. He died eleven years later, aged 83.

# INTRODUCTORY NOTE

IN an illuminating essay printed in another volume of this series Mr Philip Guedalla has called Mr Belloc "a panorama," and hinted at the same time that there are too many of him. The amazing versatility of the man certainly does much to justify this view. Poet and journalist, historian and geographer, military expert and Member of Parliament—Mr Belloc is, or has been, all these, and yet the tale of his accomplishments is far from told. And there would be no greater mistake than to suppose that the marvellous range of his achievement gives an indication of shallowness. At its best his prose stands unsurpassed in our day, and he has been credited with having written one of the perfect poems in the English language. To understand Mr Belloc aright, however, one must perceive that under all this embarrassing diversity there is a consistent oneness of purpose. The many roads have a single objective. No man is more singleminded: none more sure of his own convictions. And that in a time when so many do not quite know what they think makes Mr Belloc stand out from among his fellows. You know what he will say on a given question, though you never can tell how he will set about it. He may elect to give you a battle-scene or a travel-sketch, nonsense rhymes or a novel—the purport remains the same. And no one can convey more skilfully the romance of the past or the mystery of high places. No writer has a keener sense of the magical colour of words coupled with a nicer economy in their use.

# HILAIRE BELLOC

Mr Belloc was born near Paris in 1870, and was brought up in Sussex, whose praises he has chanted so lustily. He served for a time in the French army, and took his degree at Oxford. That, as a beginning, gave promise of a career of unusual interest, and that promise has certainly not been unfulfilled.

Thanks are due to Messrs Thomas Nelson and Sons, Ltd., for permission to reprint " The Fog," from *The Path to Rome*, " Valmy," from *The Girondin*, and " The Second of November, 1902," from *The Four Men* ; to Messrs Gerald Duckworth and Co., Ltd., for " Ronsard," from *Avril*, and " Barbary," from *Esto Perpetua* ; and to Messrs T. N. Foulis for " London River," from *The River of London*.

F. H. P.

# CONTENTS

# THE FOG

THE Brienzer Grat is an extraordinary thing. It is quite straight; its summits are, of course, of different heights, but from below they seem even, like a ridge: and, indeed, the whole mountain is more like a ridge than any other I have seen. At one end is a peak called the " Red Horn," the other end falls suddenly above Interlaken. It is as steep as anything can be short of sheer rock. There are no precipices on it, though there are nasty slabs quite high enough to kill a man— I saw several of three or four hundred feet. It is about five or six thousand feet high, and it stands right up and along the northern shore of the lake of Brienz. I began the ascent.

Spongy meads, that soughed under the feet and grew steeper as one rose, took up the first few hundred feet. Little rivulets of mere dampness ran in among the under moss, and such very small hidden flowers as there were drooped with the surfeit of moisture. The rain was now indistinguishable from a mist, and indeed I had come so near to the level belt of cloud, that already its gloom was exchanged for that diffused light which fills vapours from within and lends them their mystery. A belt of thick brushwood and low trees lay before me, clinging to the slope, and as I pushed with great difficulty and many turns to right and left through its tangle a wisp of cloud enveloped me, and from that time on I was now in, now out, of a deceptive drifting fog, in which it was most difficult to gauge one's progress.

Now and then a higher mass of rock, a peak on the ridge, would show clear through a corridor of cloud and be hidden again; also at times I would stand hesitating before a sharp wall or slab, and wait for a shifting of the fog to make sure of the best way round. I struck what might have been a loose path or perhaps only a gully; lost it again and found it again. In one place I climbed up a jagged surface for fifty feet, only to find when it cleared that it was no part of the general ascent, but a mere obstacle which might have been outflanked. At another time I stopped for a good quarter of an hour at an edge that might have been an indefinite fall of smooth rock, but that turned out to be a short drop, easy for a man, and not much longer than my body. So I went upwards always, drenched and doubting, and not sure of the height I had reached at any time.

At last I came to a place where a smooth stone lay between two pillared monoliths, as though it had been put there for a bench. Though all around me was dense mist, yet I could see above me the vague shape of a summit looming quite near. So I said to myself—

" I will sit here and wait till it grows lighter and clearer, for I must now be within two or three hundred feet of the top of the ridge, and as anything at all may be on the other side, I had best go carefully and knowing my way."

So I sat down facing the way I had to go and looking upwards, till perhaps a movement of the air might show me against a clear sky the line of the ridge, and so let me estimate the work that remained to do. I kept my eyes fixed on the point where I judged the sky-line to lie, lest I should miss some sudden gleam revealing it; and as I sat there I grew mournful and began to consider the folly of climbing this great height on an empty stomach. The soldiers of the Republic fought their battles often before breakfast, but never, I think, without having drunk warm coffee, and no one should

10

attempt great efforts without some such refreshment before starting. Indeed, my fasting, and the rare thin air of the height, the chill and the dampness that had soaked my thin clothes through and through, quite lowered my blood and left it *piano*, whimpering, and irresolute. I shivered and demanded the sun.

Then I bethought me of the hunk of bread I had stolen, and pulling it out of my haversack I began to munch that ungrateful breakfast. It was hard and stale, and gave me little sustenance; I still gazed upwards into the uniform meaningless light fog, looking for the ridge.

Suddenly, with no warning to prepare the mind, a faint but distinct wind blew upon me, the mist rose in a wreath backward and upward, and I was looking through clear immensity, not at any ridge, but over an awful gulf at great white fields of death. The Alps were right upon me and before me, overwhelming and commanding empty downward distances of air. Between them and me was a narrow dreadful space of nothingness and silence, and a sheer mile below us both, a floor to that prodigious hollow, lay the little lake.

My stone had not been a halting-place at all, but was itself the summit of the ridge, and those two rocks on either side of it framed a notch upon the very edge and sky-line of the high hills of Brienz.

Surprise and wonder had not time to form in my spirit before both were swallowed up by fear. The proximity of that immense wall of cold, the Alps, seen thus full from the level of its middle height and comprehended as it cannot be from the depths; its suggestion of something never changing throughout eternity—yet dead—was a threat to the eager mind. They, the vast Alps, all wrapped round in ice, frozen, and their immobility enhanced by the delicate, roaming veils which (as from an attraction) hovered in their hollows, seemed to halt the process of living. And the living soul whom they thus perturbed was supported by no companionship. There were no trees or blades of grass around me, only the uneven and primal stones of that height. There were no birds in the gulf; there was no sound. And the whiteness of the glaciers, the blackness of the snow-streaked rocks beyond, was glistening and unsoftened. There had come something evil into their sublimity. I was afraid.

Nor could I bear to look downwards. The slope was in no way a danger. A man could walk up it without often using his hands, and a man could go down it slowly without any direct fall, though here and there he would have to turn round at each dip or step and hold with his hands and feel a little for his foothold. I suppose the general slope, down, down, to where the green began was not sixty degrees, but have you ever tried looking down five thousand feet at sixty degrees? It drags the mind after it, and I could not bear to begin the descent.

However, I reasoned with myself. I said to myself that a man should only be afraid of real dangers. That nightmare was not for the daylight. That there was now no mist, but a warm sun. Then choosing a gully where water sometimes ran, but now dry, I warily began to descend, using my staff and leaning well backwards.

There was this disturbing thing about the gully, that it went in steps, and before each step one saw the sky just a yard or two ahead: one lost the comforting sight of earth. One knew of course that it would only be a little drop, and that the slope would begin again, but it disturbed one. And it is a trial to drop or clamber down, say fourteen or fifteen feet, sometimes twenty, and then to find no flat foothold but that eternal steep beginning again.

I went very slowly. When I was about half-way down and had come to a place where a shoulder of heaped rock stood on my left and where little parallel ledges led up to it, having grown accustomed to the descent and easier in my mind, I sat down on a slab and drew imperfectly the things I saw: the lake below me, the first forests clinging to the foot of the Alps beyond, their higher slopes of snow, and the clouds that had now begun to gather round them and that altogether hid the last third of their enormous height.

Then I saw a steamer on the lake. I felt in touch with men. The slope grew easier. I snapped my fingers at the great devils that haunt high mountains. I sniffed the gross and comfortable air of the lower valleys. I entered the belt of wood and was soon going quite a pace through the trees, for I had found a path, and was now able to sing. So I did.

At last I saw through the trunks, but a few hundred feet below me, the highroad that skirts the lake. I left the path and scrambled straight down to it. I came to a wall which I climbed, and found myself in somebody's garden. Crossing this and admiring its wealth and order (I was careful not to walk on the lawns), I opened a little private gate and came on to the road, and from there to Brienz was but a short way along a fine hard surface in a hot morning sun, with the gentle lake on my right hand not five yards away, and with delightful trees upon my left, caressing and sometimes even covering me with their shade.

I was therefore dry, ready, and contented when I entered by mid-morning the curious town of Brienz, which is all one long street, and of which the population is Protestant. I say dry, ready, and contented; dry in my clothes, ready for food, contented with men and nature. But as I entered I squinted up that

HILAIRE BELLOC

interminable slope, I saw the fog wreathing again along the ridge so infinitely above me, and I considered myself a fool to have crossed the Brienzer Grat without breakfast. But I could get no one in Brienz to agree with me, because no one thought I had done it, though several people there could talk French.

*From " The Path to Rome "*

# RONSARD

I F it be true that words create for themselves a special atmosphere, and that their mere sound calls up vague outer things beyond their strict meaning, so it is true that the names of the great poets by their mere sound, by something more than the recollection of their work, produce an atmosphere corresponding to the quality of each; and the name of Ronsard throws about itself like an aureole the characters of fecundity, of leadership, and of fame.

A group of men to which allusion will be made in connexion with Du Bellay set out with a programme, developed a determined school, and fixed the literary renaissance of France at its highest point. They steeped themselves in antiquity, and they put to the greatest value it has ever received the name of poet; they demanded that the poet should be a kind of king, or seer. Half seriously, half as a product of mere scholarship, the pagan conception of the muse and of inspiration filled them.

More than that; in their earnest, and, as it seemed at first, artificial work, they formed the French language. Some of its most famous and most familiar words proceed from them—for instance, the word *Patrie*. Some few of their exotic Greek and Latin adaptations were dropped; the greater part remained. They have excluded from French—as some think to the impoverishment of that language—most elements of the Gothic— the inversion of the adjective, the frequent suppression of the relative, the irregularity of form, which had survived from the Middle Ages, and which make the older

French poetry so much more sympathetic to the Englishman than is the new—all these were destroyed by the group of men of whom I speak. They were called by their contemporaries the Pléiade, for they were seven stars.

Now, of these, Ronsard was easily the master. He had that power which our anæmic age can hardly comprehend, of writing, writing, writing, without fear of exhaustion, without irritability or self-criticism, without danger of comparing the better with the worse. Five great volumes of small print, all good—men of that facility never write the really paltry things—all good, and most of it glorious; some of it on the level which only the great poets reach here and there. It is in reading this man who rhymed unceasingly for forty years, who made of poetry an occupation as well as a glory, and who let it fill the whole of his life, that one feels how much such creative power has to do with the value of verse. There is a kind of good humility about it, the humility of a man who does not look too closely at himself, and the health of a soul at full stride, going forward. You may open Ronsard at any page, and find a beauty; you may open any one of the sonnets at random, and in translating it discover that you are compelled to a fine English, because he is saying, plainly, great things. And of these sonnets, note you, he would write thirty at a stretch, and then twenty, and then a second book, with seventy more. So that as one reads one cannot help understanding that Italian who said a man was no poet unless he could rap out a century of sonnets from time to time; and one is reminded of the general vigour of the age and of the way in which art of all sorts was mingled up together, when one remembers the tags of verses, just such verses as these, which are yet to be seen in our galleries set down doubtfully

16

on the margin of their sketches by the great artists of
Italy.

Ronsard, with these qualities of a leader, unconscious,
as all true leaders are, of the causes of his leadership, and
caring, as all true leaders do, for nothing in leadership
save the glory it brings with it, had also, as have all
leaders, chiefly the power of drawing in a multitude of
friends. The peculiar head of his own group, he very
soon became the head of all the movement of his day.
He had made letters really great in the minds of his
contemporaries, and having so made them, appeared
before them as a master of those letters. Certainly, as
I shall quote him in a moment when I come to his
dying speech, he was " satiated with glory."

Yet this man did not in his personality convey that
largeness which was his principal mark. His face was
narrow, long, and aquiline; his health uneven. It was
evidently his soul which made men quickly forget the
ill-matched case which bore it; for almost alone of the
great poets he was consistently happy, and there poured
out from him not only this unceasing torrent of verse,
but also advice, sustenance, and a kind of secondary
inspiration for others.

In yet another matter he was a leader, and a leader of
the utmost weight, not the cause, perhaps, but certainly
the principal example of the trend which the mind of
the nation was taking as the sixteenth century drew to
a close. I mean in the matter of religion, upon whose
colour every society depends, which is the note even of
a national language, and which seems to be the ultimate
influence beyond which no historical analysis can carry
a thinking man.

But even those who will not admit the truth of this
should watch the theory closely, for with the religious
trend of France is certainly bound up, and, as I would

maintain, on such an influence is dependent, that ultimate setting of the French classic, that winding up of the Renaissance, with which I shall deal in the essay upon Malherbe.

The stream of Catholicism was running true. The nation was tumbling back after a high and turbulent flood into the channel it had scoured for itself by the unbroken energies of a thousand years. It is no accident that Ronsard, that Du Bellay, were churchmen. It is a type. It is a type of the truth that the cloth admitted poets; of the truth that in the great battle whose results yet trouble Europe, here, on the soil where the great questions are fought out, Puritanism was already killed. The epicurean in them both, glad and ready in Ronsard, sombre and Lucretian in Du Bellay, jarred indeed in youth against their vows; but that it should have been tolerated, that it should have led to no excess or angry revolt, was typical of their moment. It was typical, finally, of their generation that all this mixture of the Renaissance with the Church matured at last into its natural fruit, for in the case of Ronsard we have a noble expression of perfect Christianity at the end.

In the November of 1585 he felt death upon him; he had himself borne to his home as soon as the Huguenot bands had left it, ravaged and devastated as it was. He found it burned and looted, but it reminded him of childhood and of the first springs of his great river of verse. A profound sadness took him. He was but in his sixty-second year, his mind had not felt any chill of age. He could not sleep; poppies and soporifics failed him. He went now in his coach, now on a litter from place to place in that countryside which he had rendered famous, and saw the Vendomois for the last time; its cornfields all stubble under a cold and dreary sky. And in each place he waited for a while.

But death troubled him, and he could not remain. Within a fortnight he ordered that they should carry him southward to the Loire, to that priory of which—by a custom of privilege, nobility, and royal favour—he was the nominal head, the priory which is "the eye and delight of Touraine"—the Isle of St Cosmo. He sickened as he went. The thirty miles or so took him three painful days; twice, all his strength failed him, and he lay half fainting in his carriage; to so much energy and to so much power of creation these episodes were an awful introduction of death.

It was upon the 17th of November that he reached the walls wherein he was Superior; six weeks later, on the second day after Christmas, he died.

Were I to describe that scene to which he called the monks, all men of his own birth and training, were I to dwell upon the appearance and the character of the oldest and the wisest, who was also the most famous there, I should extend this essay beyond its true limit, as I should also do were I to write down, even briefly, the account of his just, resigned, and holy death. It must suffice that I transcribe the chief of his last deeds; I mean, that declaration wherein he made his last profession of faith.

The old monk had said to him: " In what resolution do you die? "

He answered, somewhat angrily: " In what did you think? In the religion which was my father's and his father's, and his father's and his father's before him—for I am of that kind."

Then he called all the community round him, as though the monastic simplicity had returned (so vital is the Faith, so simple its primal energies), and as though he had been the true prior of some early and fervent house, he told them these things which I will faithfully

19

translate on account of their beauty. They are printed here, I think, for the first time in English, and must stand for the end of this essay:

He said: "That he had sinned like other men, and, perhaps, more than most; that his senses had led him away by their charm, and that he had not repressed or constrained them as he should; but none the less, he had always held that Faith which the men of his line had left him, he had always clasped close the Creed and the unity of the Catholic Church; that, in fine, he had laid a sure foundation, but he had built thereon with wood, with hay, with straw. As for that foundation, he was sure it would stand; as for the light and worthless things he had built upon it he had trust in the mercy of the Saviour that they would be burnt in the fire of His love. And now he begged them all to believe hard, as he had believed; but not to live as he had lived; they must understand that he had never attempted or plotted against the life or goods of another, nor ever against any man's honour, but, after all, there was nothing therein wherewith to glorify one's self before God." When he had wept a little, he continued, saying, "that the world was a ceaseless turmoil and torment, and shipwreck after shipwreck all the while, and a whirlpool of sins, and tears and pain, and that to all these misfortunes there was but one port, and this port was Death. But, as for him, he carried with him into that port no desire and no regret for life. That he had tried every one of its pretended joys, that he had left nothing undone which could give him the least shadow of pleasure or content, but that at the end he had found everywhere the oracle of Wisdom, vanity of vanities."

He ended with this magnificent thing, which is, perhaps, the last his human power conceived, and I will put it down in his own words:

" Of all those vanities, the loveliest and most praise-worthy is glory—fame. No one of my time has been so filled with it as I; I have lived in it, and loved and triumphed in it through time past, and now I leave it to my country to garner and possess it after I shall die. So do I go away from my own place as satiated with the glory of this world as I am hungry and all longing for that of God."

*From "Avril"*

# THE APPRENTICE

### *January* 30, 1649

MEN were well into the working week; it was a Tuesday and apprentices were under the hard eyes of their masters throughout the City of London and in the rarer business places that elbowed the great palaces along the Strand. The sky was overcast and the air distastefully cold, nor did anything in the landscape seem colder than the dark band of the river under those colourless and lifeless January clouds.

Whether it were an illusion or a reality, one could have sworn that there was a sort of silence over the houses and on the families of the people; one could have sworn that men spoke in lower tones than was their custom, and that the streets were emptier. The trial and the sentence of the King had put all that great concourse of men into the very presence of Death.

The day wore on; the noise of the workmen could be heard at the scaffold by Whitehall; one hour was guessed at and then another; rumours and flat assertions were busy everywhere, especially among the young, and an apprentice to a harness-maker in the Water Lane near Essex House knew not what to believe. But he was determined to choose his moment and to slip away lest he should miss so great a sight. The tyranny of the army kept all the city in doubt all day long, and allowed no news; none the less, from before noon there had begun a little gathering of people in Whitehall, round the scaffold at which men were still giving the last strokes of the hammer. Somewhat after noon a horse-shoe of cavalry assembled in their long cloaks and

22

curious tall civilian hats; they stood ranked, with swords drawn, all round the platform. Their horses shifted uneasily in the cold.

The harness-maker's apprentice found his opportunity; his master was called to the door for an order from Arundel House, and the lad left his bench quickly, just as he was, without hat or coat, in the bitter weather, and darting through the side door ran down through the Water Gate and down its steps to the river. The tide was at the flood and his master's boat lay moored. He cast her off and pulled rapidly up the line of gardens, backing water when he came to the public stairs just beyond Whitehall. Here he quickly tied the painter and ran up breathless to Whitehall Gate, fearing he might have missed his great expectation. He was in ample time.

It was perhaps half-past three o'clock when he got through the gate and found himself in the press of people. Far off to the left, among the soldiery that lined the avenue from the Park to the Mall, and so to St James', a continuous roll of drums burdened the still air.

The crowd was not very large, but it filled the space from the gate to the scaffold and a little beyond, save where it was pressed outward by the ring of cavalry. It did not overflow into the wide spaces of the park, though these lay open to Whitehall, nor did it run up towards Charing Cross beyond the Banqueting Hall.

The apprentice was not so tall as the men about him; he strained and elbowed a little to see, and he was sworn at. He could make out the low scaffold, a large platform all draped in black, with iron staples, and a railing round it; it covered the last three blank windows of Whitehall, running from the central casement until it met the brick house at the north end of the stonework; there the brickwork beneath one of the windows had been taken out so as to give access through it from the floor within to the scaffold on the same level without; and whispers round told the apprentice, though he did not know how much to trust them, that it was through this hasty egress that the King would appear. Upon the scaffold itself stood a group of men, two of them masked, and one of the masked ones, of great stature and strong, leant upon the axe with his arm crossed upon the haft of it. A little block, barely raised above the floor of the platform, he could only see by leaping on tiptoe, catching it by glimpses between the heads of his neighbours or the shoulders of the cavalry guard; but he noticed in those glimpses how very low it was, and saw, ominous upon it, two staples driven as though to contain the struggler. Before it, so that one kneeling would have his face toward the Palace and away from the crowd, was a broad footstool covered with red velvet, and making a startling patch upon all that expanse of black baize.

It was cold waiting; the motionless twigs of the small bare trees in the Park made it seem colder still. The three-quarters struck in the new clock behind him upon Whitehall Gate, but as yet no one had appeared.

In a few moments, however, there was a movement in the crowd, heads turning to the right, and a corresponding backing of the mounted men to contain the first beginnings of a rush, for the commanders of the army feared, while they despised, the popular majority of London; and the wealthy merchants, the allies of the army, had not joined this common lot. This turning of faces towards the great blank stone wall of the Palace was caused by a sound of many footsteps within. The only window not masked with stone, the middle window, was that upon which their gaze universally

24

turned. They saw, passing it very rapidly, a group of men within; they were walking very sharply along the floor (which was here raised above the level of the window itself and cut the lower panes of it); they were hurrying towards the northern end of the great Banqueting Hall. It was but a moment's vision, and again they appeared in the open air through the broken brickwork at the far end of the stone façade.

For a moment the apprentice saw clearly the slight King, his face grown old, his pointed beard left full, his long features not moved. The great cloak that covered him, with the Great Star of the Garter upon the left shoulder, he drew off quickly and let fall into the hands of Herbert. He wore no hat; he stepped forward with precision towards the group of executioners, and a little murmur ran through the crowd.

The old Bishop, moving his limbs with difficulty, but suppliant and attendant upon his friend, stood by in an agony. He helped the King to pull off his inner coat until he stood conspicuous in the sky-blue vest beneath it, and round his neck a ribbon and one ornament upon it, a George carved in onyx. This also he removed and gave to the Bishop, while he took from his hands a little white silken cap and fixed it firmly upon his long and beautiful hair. From beneath the sky blue of his garment, at the neck and at the wrists, appeared frills of exquisite linen and the adornment of lace. He stood for a few moments praying, then turned and spoke as though he were addressing them all. But the apprentice, though he held his breath and strained to hear, as did all others about him, could catch no separate word, but only the general sound of the King's voice speaking. The movement of the horses, the occasional striking of a hoof upon the setts of the street, the distance, covered that voice. Next Charles was saying something to the masked man, and a moment later he was kneeling upon the footstool. The apprentice saw him turn a moment and spread his arms out as an example of what he next should do; he bent him toward the block—it was too low; he lay at full length, and the crowd lifted and craned to see him in this posture.

The four heavy strokes of the hour struck and boomed in the silence. The hands of the lying figure were stretched out again, this time as a final signal, and right up in the air above them all the axe swung, white against the grey sky, flashed and fell.

In a moment the group upon the scaffold had closed round, a cloth was thrown, the body was raised, and among the hands stretched out to it were the eager and enfeebled hands of the Bishop, trembling and still grasping the George.

A long moan or wail, very strange and dreadful, not very loud, rose from the people now that their tension was slackened by the accomplishment of the deed. And at once from the north and from the south, with such ceremony as is used to the conquered, the cavalry charged right through, hacking and dispersing these Londoners and driving them every way.

The apprentice dodged and ran, his head full of the tragedy and bewildered, his body in active fear of the horses that pursued flying packets of the crowd down the alley-ways of the offices and Palace buildings.

He went off by a circuitous way to find, not his master's house after such an escapade, but his mother's, where she lived beyond St Martin's.

The dusk did not long tarry; as it gathered and turned to night small flakes of snow began to fall and lie upon the frozen ground.

*From " The Eye-witness "*

# VALMY

THE day dawned after that night of pitiless rain and mud; the drowned and miserable light, the half-light of the hopeless morning, showed nothing but bare fields in which small stunted trees shivered under the steady drizzle. The column was checked somewhere ahead, the old white horse halted abruptly; Boutroux, lolling in his saddle, was jolted out of his sleep. He straightened himself and was awake.

"The longer I live," he muttered to his wretched mount, "the more I learn! Get up, my poor beast. A man can sleep in the saddle fasting and under a shower-bath. It would astonish them at home!"

As the word crossed his lips he had a sharp vision within him—too sharp, the illusion of fasting and fatigue. He saw the Gironde under the sunlight, the quay, the old and noble houses; his room and his books returned to him—it was sleep returning. But the old horse stumbled, and the picture disappeared. He had a friend and a reality to hand. Here was a horse who got on with him well enough. . . . But what a crock!

With that reflection he patted his unfortunate beast upon its sodden, steaming neck. But the poor victim was beyond comfort, and put one hoof before the other mechanically and with the weight of despair.

Boutroux looked round him under the dawn and saw a miserable sight:

Two miles and more of men stretched straggling along the road before him. In his own troop there was no semblance of order. The men at his side and those immediately before him were more or less his

27

companions, yet not all of the same troop. Mixed up with them in a hopeless confusion limped a few boys, their uniforms torn, one of them with a boot cracked to the sole, another with his face tied up in a chance rag which some kindly woman had lent him in a farm. He had the toothache and his cheek was swollen.

Others of the line were jumbled with the hussars; two gunners also, come from God knows where, their dark clothes plastered with mud as though they had rolled in it, their headgear too large for them, squashed down over their ears and foreheads.

Far ahead a confusion of carts struggled on through the weather, and in the marshy fields to the right a ludicrous attempt at a flanking party, a dozen horses or so, splashed and sucked as best they could through the drowned clay. Very far off forward came from time to time a loud, cursing order; and in one place near by Boutroux could see a man collapsed upon the roadside and a sergeant striking him with the butt end of a musket to make him move. But the man would not move, for he was dead. And even as Boutroux saw such a sight, after all that night and all that fatigue, he smiled, for in the sight there was something political; the sergeant was an aged man, and his regiment was a regiment with traditions, a regiment that was proud to call itself Artois. The white facings of it were dingy enough now. The sergeant of Artois abandoned his task, and Boutroux turned away his eyes. He was not used to the death of men.

So the dawn rose through and beyond the steady rain upon that large and hopeless force, making its last few miles and nearing, as it thought, its end.

As the light broadened a deep mist enveloped them all around. It was a mist through which the fine, almost imperceptible rain settled into the already sodden

28

clothes. It mercifully shut out from those discouraged and broken men all sights save their immediate duty. They passed through the streets of a village, the long weary line of them, and more than one of the line took advantage of the fog and of a break in the hustle to hide himself in a side lane in the hope of escaping what was to come. They approached a narrow tumble-down bridge at the head of which, by dint of violence, some sort of order was arranged. The men on foot were thrust back, the cavalry sent forward first, and among the first hundred Boutroux's troop of hussars, mounted anyhow and wishing they were dead. Even in that fatigue and as he passed it, Boutroux, to whom the things of the eyes were very precious, noticed that the little stream ran milk-white, and he thought it curious.

" Everything," he said to himself, " in this accursed North country is strange! "

A quarter of an hour after, at the head of the rising lane, as the hussars struggled forward, fetlock deep in mud, there loomed through the fog a line of high trees, and it was some slight comfort, after such a march, for the cavalry to find themselves on the great highroad. They were filed off by the left along it, and it was passed along from one man to another that the main camp was close by.

Seven strokes sounded from the cracked old bell of the village below: the sound came harsh and tinny yet muffled through the mist, and when the last stroke sounded the whole mysterious and obscure surroundings were shrouded again in misty silence save for the shuffling of damp feet upon damper earth as the line crawled and tumbled up pell-mell from the brook below on to the height of the road.

Suddenly all their minds and all the imagined land-scape beyond the fog was transformed for them by a sound which very few of those huddled thousands had ever heard. It was the sound which all who lived were to hear for twenty years: the unannounced, unbugled boom of guns. Far up to the left along the great highway—upon a height it seemed, from the noise—they were firing. It came and it came again—a mile away perhaps—perhaps more.

*Thud!* . . . it was the earth that carried the sound. Half a minute's silence, then again—*Thud!* . . . One could have sworn the dripping leaves upon the high, roadside trees had trembled. The less weary and the younger of the long line of horses stirred at the sound and sniffed the air. . . . *Thud!* . . . It came again.

What guns and whose had thus opened the game none but the staff could tell—but they were firing, and there was action. For some few moments an alertness and almost a gaiety came into the eyes of these young men, broken with fatigue though they were and with the ceaseless marching of the night.

Boutroux's old horse lifted its head with a faint gesture that years ago might have betrayed a recognition of that sound; but that head drooped again, and the beast stood as weary as ever in the long line of the cavalry drawn up beside the road. . . .

A fainter, less certain, a more distant noise began to answer: the enemy had opened his reply. *Thud! Thud!* . . . the nearer pieces were firing faster and faster, the further batteries opposed followed pace for pace; for an hour it grew from a measured beat to a broken roar, at last a furious cannonade.

But all that business and momentous sound was veiled; and those cannon seemed to be part of ghostly and unseen things.

No shadow of a man approached down the road through the grey murk; only now and then a slight breath of wind, rising as though lifted by the anger of the far artillery, blew a clear space before the eyes of the cavalry. In such a moment could be seen half a mile of the long road: the infantry in their ranks waiting; the wagons drawn up by the kerb; a chance group of officers with maps, watching and straining towards the sound of the firing. Then the lane, so opened for a moment, as quickly closed again with new rolls of cloud, and swallowed up in it the countryside: bare rolling land; miserable wet stubble; the white bare patches of the famine-fields, where not even rye could grow. All the while the rumble and the thunder continued.

A brigade of cavalry passed before them, and the hussars, dismounted, watched them go by with envy. They could understand no more of the welter than their fellows left behind, but at least they were going to act, and this mere halting in the rain was one more weight of despair to their less fortunate fellows.

The clatter of their shoes died away in the fog: the cannonade had dropped to a fitful exchange of shots, which at last came only from the further and more distant guns. The young men were talking to each other aimlessly; certain of the infantry, at the end of the long straggling roadside line, were too free. They had sauntered up and were speaking with their dismounted comrades of the hussars, when as sudden and as unexpected as that first cannonade, but twenty times more violent, crashing like the fall of some titanic plate of metal, or the clapping to of some vast door, rang another nearer and intolerable firing. It ceased abruptly: two minutes later a novel sound came through the fog; it was like the noise of flood waters, or of a hurricane in trees at night; it was the approach of broken men.

First a few, flying in a complete disorder, pierced through out of the fog, stopped, and tried to form again as they came upon the infantry and the cavalry lining the road. Then, as more and yet more poured upon them in the panic, they broke yet again.

So scattered, so pouring by, rallied here and there in confused groups by desperate superiors, whirling in eddies, streaming away in curses and blows and adjurations, half a brigade and more of the stampede fled down the great highway and were swallowed up in the mist again.

The hussars had barely time to note them—one officer was heard saying to another that the wreckage was from Dumouriez's lot—when yet another body came retreating down the great road, in somewhat better plight but heavily mauled.

It was followed by a maimed and jumbled pack of wagons, with limbers here and there, and here and there the carriage of a broken gun. The horses of the teams had blood upon their flanks, and more than one limber was dragged by a team from which a leader or a wheeler had been cut away, so that the end of the trace hung knotted and severed. Confused and scrambling, that deafening jostle and jolt of wheels went past in its turn; following it, the last of the broken position, and a covering for its flying defenders, walked past with more dignity and in far better order a mounted force. These also passed, and were lost in the mist beyond. The noise of the flight grew less, and ceased altogether. There came up the now empty road two orderlies galloping hard: the officers in command of the waiting roadside line received them. In a quarter of an hour the infantry and the hussars had formed into column and were off eastward again upon their endless business of unexplained advance and fatigue.

The young men had heard cannon, and had seen the

beginning of war : they were bewildered, and for the most part they remembered best, of that confused morning hour with its cries of panic and flood of fugitives rolling before them, the *coffee* hot and ample. There had been coffee and bread by the gallon. They all remembered it for many days.

Within a mile they saw through the rising mist, dimly, the spire and the houses of another village upon the great highroad; behind it a whole field of tents where the main force of Kellermann had waited through that sodden night. But the tents were striking even as they approached, and a vast mass of equipage and train was moving off on to the empty uplands above, while the heads of the columns were being wheeled each in turn off the great road towards the fields above; the hussars with the rest. The horses dragged as best they could through the morass of those ploughlands, men riding in front picked out the hardest going, and every few moments the whole winding trail of them would halt as the head of it was checked at a soft patch.

The mist shredded and grew thinner; the wind had risen. The far field line along the sky was plainer, and the soldiers began to tell one another that they were nearing a main position. Far off in the mist, behind them at first, but on their left as the long line of men wheeled northward, sounded fitfully and unseen and muffled the distant guns of the invaders.

The head of the hussars had reached a crest, the infantry had already occupied its further side, when there came down the irregular mass shouted orders that struck and halted the joints of the column: the two miles of men were to stand.

It was ten o'clock when the halt came. Till noon there was no further movement. The hussars had dismounted again; the fog rose lighter and lighter yet;

c                                                          33 the wind strengthened and scattered it over great patches of dull landscape; here and there a mass of distant men, the enemy, appeared westward from the height on which the cavalry stood.

Boutroux and his troop were holding their mounts to the leeward of a great windmill which stood up, sheltering them somewhat from the weather; into the depth of that weather the ill-formed thousands of the army extended, all at haphazard. Beside the mill and along the crest before it were drawn up the foot in every form. Boutroux, from behind his shelter of the mill, saw with a complete indifference battery after battery, six batteries in all, get slowly through the press, and have a way made for them to positions on the ridge of the hill.

All behind the mill and on either side was a confusion of men, chiefly of the mounted forces, scattered pell-mell. On the same sheltered side of the hill lay little packs of men who had fallen out, and the few wounded, and there were groups of sappers as well. Here and there a bunch of the Grenadiers in their tall bearskins; the mass of cavalry waiting dismounted, and the whole of this reserve without due form or order.

It was noon, and there was nothing forward. Boutroux considered within himself how strange a thing was active service, and how incomprehensible a thing a battle—if indeed this was battle, and battle it surely was, to judge by the perpetual distant cannonade. He guessed vaguely what might be the plan; abandoned the muddled riddle, and did not even ask his old white horse for aid in such a problem. He crouched there in the lee of the mill, watching the haggard and empty faces of the idle groups about him, wondering what might be doing on the edge of the crest beyond his shelter, watching a barrel of wine slowly dragged up upon two wheels by a donkey, which a most hideous

34

canteen woman of the 98th was leading with difficulty, and blows, through the mud

All the while the distant guns kept up their ceaseless and repeated booming, and now and then a shell fell wide over the heads of them all, to drop in the further valley and be lost in the mist of it, and now and then a luckier aim dropped a solid shot not far from the mill walls, so that the ground shook with it. Sometimes, much more rarely, some stroke of even better fortune for the enemy, or of better aim at a moment when the wind was steady, would make a dance near by: a clatter of breakage and a slamming blow, followed by a scuffle and cries.

But still—there was very little doing. Boutroux munched his bread, and gazed on the reserves before him. He saw only a lot of most unfortunate men, drenched as though they had swum through a pond; a great welter of horses also, of wagons, and here and there of provisionment; the smoke of a fire where some one had lit it for the warming of his coffee in spite of the weather, and the occasional whistle and thud of projectiles falling near at hand, set to the irregular, distant, and sullen boom of the enemy's guns.

Then, as noon turned, the guns of his own forces took it up—they were not a hundred yards behind him; they shook the air, and the ground, and all his bones. He thought the noise intolerable—it was just beyond the mill, blasting him to pieces every quarter of a minute, and drowning all his senses. But he had to bear it, had Boutroux—and as for the old white horse, he cared as little for the nearer as he had cared for the further noise.

The wind was rising, the mist had turned into low clouds that scurried before it. There was now neither mist nor drizzle, though the air was very cold; the intervals of open sky grew larger and more frequent, and sunlight—for the first time in all those dreadful days—broke upon the tarnished colours of the force. A man strolled up to Boutroux and told him it was worth seeing.

"Worth seeing—what?" said Boutroux.

"They're beginning to advance," he said. He told Boutroux that from a place a little way back, where there was a gap, one could see everything. But Boutroux didn't want to see: he would stick it out where he was with his horse, in the lee of the mill. The whole thing was quite beyond him.

All the while that damaging and rocking noise of the French guns tormented and bewildered the air. He heard loud shouts of command—the staggering line beyond the mill was suffering some sort of order; it was massing into three columns. He could see linesmen called up from scattered groups and hurriedly shifting their packs on to their shoulders. He could see men running to take their places in the tail of companies. Then, during a pause in that incessant firing, he heard a great volley of cheers, and the confused political cries, enthusiastic and young, which reminded him of the street rows at home.

His curiosity got the better of him. He hooked his bridle to the mill door staple, peeped round the corner of the brickwork—and saw nothing. . . . At least only those three great masses of men, all solemnly drawn up together.

They hid from Boutroux the guns that were massed in front, on the edge of the hill, but he did see for one moment Kellermann and his staff mounted and showing high above the line. And as the general rode down the front, just before the sight of him was lost in the press beyond Boutroux saw him leading and answering the

36

cheers, the three-coloured plume of his hat waved on the point of his sword.

Having so seen, Boutroux went back to his shelter and tried to bear the noise. He was about to soften its terrors by further gentle conversation with his mount, when a crash so very much more abominable than all he had yet heard drove from him the memory of name and place and time. The whole fabric of the mill shivered, the air was a moment stunned and dead . . . the dreadful pause of a second, no more, was followed by a dense cloud of black and pungent smoke blowing before the high wind past either side of the building, and in the same moment came up that terrible unnumbered cry of many wounded men, shrieking and rising pointed upon a background of yet more terrible moans. He heard articulate appeals for death, and next, immediately, he saw great lumps of the linesmen crouching, turning, hiding, in every attitude; a moment later and a whole brigade was flying past him, with officers and sergeants cursing in German, striking and wounding and turning the cattle back with the sword—it was the German mercenaries maddened by the explosion of the limbers, and roaring for safety from such hells. Boutroux was like a man moored to the pier of a bridge during the swell of a flood; he was protected from that flood of war by the brickwork of the mill, but he was enclosed with swirls of panic on every side.

It was soon over. They got the paid men under control as one gets a fire under control. The mass was beaten and salved into shape; it shuffled back into some sort of order again, and one troop after another of cavalry were got together and sent forward. The hussars were still left alone, and empty of business in the shelter of the hill. No orders came for them. A fatigue came up (on the crest beyond, the guns still hammered and banged); it came staggering under a great measure of oats. It was high time, and Boutroux very contentedly filled his poor beast's nose-bag and tied it on. At first the old white horse would not eat, but Boutroux coaxed :

" I have no wine for you," he said; " but if you will eat, like a good beast, I will steal water for you from the gunners."

The guns went on with their dance more furiously than ever. Now and then an isolated cheer broke out, recalling to Boutroux that first storm of cheers when Kellermann had rallied the line two hours before. Now and then the sharp break of a shell, the noise and cries of it, or the ground far before him caught by a chance shot, startled him. The guns went on. Boutroux was almost grown part of the deafening on the other side of his mill; he had almost forgotten what a day was like in which there were no guns . . . yet these were the first guns he had ever known. The thing comes quickly.

Hour after hour throughout the afternoon that noise occupied the sky, until at last, at about five (at any rate, his stomach, though shaken by the fire, told him it was the time for soup), the slow dropping of the cannonade became more and more marked to the listener.

As the fitful and rarer shots succeeded one another, the mist, now wholly blown away, the open sky which had followed it, were in turn succeeded, perhaps as a sequence to so terrible a duel, by a black ceiling of storm; the last vengeance of that fortnight's weather poured angrily upon the thousands massed and huddled round the mill, passed, and it was clear again. No further battery fired, save, very far off to the northward, one stray shot and then another. The cannonade was done.

*From " The Girondin "*

# BARBARY

WHEN a man first sees Africa, if it is just before the rising of the sun, he perceives, right up against a clean horizon, what appear to be islands standing out distinct and sharp above the sea.

At this hour a wind is often blowing from the eastward, and awakens the Mediterranean as though it came purposely at dawn to make the world ready for the morning. The little waves leap up beneath it, steep towards their shadows, and the bows of the ship that had surged all night through a rolling calm begin, as sailors say, to 'speak': the broken water claps and babbles along the side. In this way, if he has good fortune, the traveller comes upon a new land. It is that land, shut off from all the rest between the desert and the sea, which the Arabs call the Island of the West, the Maghreb, but to which we in Europe for many hundred years have given the name of Barbary: as it says in the song about freedom:

> . . . as large as a Lion reclined
> By the rivers of Barbary.

It is the shore that runs, all built upon a single plan, from Tunis and the Gulf of Carthage to Tangier; that was snatched from Europe in one great cavalry charge twelve hundred years ago, and is now at last again in the grasp of Europe.

For many hours the traveller will sail towards it until at last he comes to a belt of smooth water which, in such weather, fringes all that coast, and then he finds that what he saw at morning was not a line of islands, but the tops of high hills standing in a range along the sea:

they show darker against a stronger light and a more southerly sun as he draws nearer, and beyond them he sees far off inland the first buttress mountains which hold up the plateaux of Atlas.

The country which he thus approaches differs in its fortune and history from all others in the world. The soil and the relief of the Maghreb, coupled with its story, have made it peculiar and, as it were, a symbol of the adventures of Europe. Ever since our Western race began its own life and entered into its ceaseless struggle against the East, this great bastion has been held and lost again; occupied by our enemies and then taken back as our power re-arose. The Phœnician ruled it; Rome wrested it back; it fell for the last time when the Roman Empire declined; its reconquest has been the latest fruit of our recovery.

It is thoroughly our own. The race that has inhabited it from its origin and still inhabits it is our race; its climate and situation are ours; it is at the furthest limit from Asia; it is an opposing shore of our inland sea; it links Sicily to Spain; it retains in every part of it the Menhirs and the Dolmens, the great stones at which our people sacrificed when they began to be men: yet even in the few centuries of written history foreign gods have twice been worshipped there and foreign rulers have twice held it for such long spaces of time that twice its nature has been forgotten. Even to-day, when our reoccupation seems assured, we speak of it as though it were by some right originally Oriental, and by some destiny certain to remain so. During the many centuries of our decline and of our slow resurrection, these countries were first cut off so suddenly and so clean from Christendom, next steeped so long and so thoroughly in an alien religion and habit of law, that their very dress and language changed; and until a man has recognized at last the faces beneath the turbans, and has seen and grown familiar with the great buildings which Rome nowhere founded more solidly than in these provinces, he is deceived by the tradition of an immediate past and by the externals of things: he sees nothing but Arabs around him, and feels himself an intruder from a foreign world.

Of this Eastern spirit, which is still by far the strongest to be found in the states of Barbary, an influence meets one long before one has made land. The little ships all up and down the Mediterranean, and especially as one nears the African coast, are in their rig and their whole manner Arabian.

There is a sort of sail which may be called the original of all sails. It is the sail with which antiquity was familiar. It brought the ships to Tenedos and the Argo carried it. The Norwegians had it when they were pirates a thousand years ago. They have it still. It is nearer a lug-sail than anything else, and indeed our Deal luggers carry something very near it. It is almost a square sail, but the yard has a slight rake and there is a bit of a peak to it. It is the kind of sail which seems to come first into the mind of any man when he sets out to use the wind. It is to be seen continually to-day hoisted above small boats in the north of Europe.

But this sail is too simple. It will not go close to the wind, and in those light and variable airs which somehow have no force along the deck, it hangs empty and makes no way because it has no height.

Now when during that great renaissance of theirs in the seventh century the Arabs left their deserts and took to the sea, they became for a short time in sailing, as in philosophy, the teachers of their new subjects. They took this sail which they had found in all the ports they had conquered along this coast—in Alexandria, in

Cyrene, in Carthage, in Cæsarea—they lightened and lengthened the yard, they lifted the peak up high, they clewed down the foot, and very soon they had that triangular *lateen* sail which will, perhaps, remain when every other evidence of their early conquering energy has disappeared. With such a sail they drove those first fleets of theirs which gave them at once the islands and the commerce of the Mediterranean. It was the sail which permitted their invasion of the northern shores and the unhappy subjection of Spain.

We Europeans have for now some seven hundred years, from at least the Third Crusade, so constantly used this gift of Islam that we half forget its origin. You may see it in all the Christian harbours of the Mediterranean to-day, in every port of the Portuguese coast, and here and there as far north as the Channel. It is not to be seen beyond Cherbourg, but in Cherbourg it is quite common. The harbour-boats that run between the fleet and the shore hoist these lateens. Yet it is not of our own making, and, indeed, it bears a foreign mark which is very distinct, and which puzzles every northerner when first he comes across this sail: it reefs along the yard. Why it should do so neither history nor the men that handle it can explain, since single sails are manifestly made to reef from the foot to the leach, where a man can best get at them. Not so the lateen. If you carry too much canvas and the wind is pressing her you must take it in from aloft, or, it must be supposed, lower the whole on deck. And this foreign, quaint, unusual thing which stamps the lateen everywhere is best seen when the sail is put away in harbour. It does not lie down along the deck as do ours in the north, but right up along the yard, and the yard itself is kept high at the masthead, making a great bow across the sky, and (one would say) tempting Providence

42

to send a gale and wreck it. Save for this mark—which may have its uses, but seems to have none and to be merely barbaric—the lateen is perfect in its kind, and might be taken with advantage throughout the world (as it is throughout all this united sea) for the uniform sail. For this kind of sail is, for small craft, the neatest and the swiftest in the world, and, in a general way, will lie closer to the wind than any other. Our own fore-and-aft rig is nothing else but a lateen cut up into mainsail, foresail, and jib, for the convenience of handling.

The little ships, so rigged, come out like heralds far from the coast to announce the old dominion of the East and of the religion that made them: of the united civilization that has launched them over all its seas, from east of India to south of Zanzibar and right out here in the western place which we are so painfully recovering. They are the only made thing, the only *form* we accepted from the Arab: and we did well to accept it. The little ships are a delight.

You see them everywhere. They belong to the sea and they animate it. They were similar as waves are similar: they are different as waves are different. They come into a hundred positions against the light. They heel and run with every mode of energy.

There is nothing makes a man's heart so buoyant as to see one of the little ships bowling along breast-high towards him, with the wind and the clouds behind it, careering over the sea. It seems to have borrowed something of the air and something of the water, and to unite them both and to be their offspring and also their bond. When they are middle-way over the sea towards one under a good breeze, the little ships are things to remember.

So it is when they carry double sail and go, as we say of our schooners, "wing and wing." For they can

43

carry two sails when the wind is moderate, and especially when the vessel is running before it, but these two sails are not carried upon two masts, but both upon the same mast. The one is the common or working sail, carried in all weathers. The other is a sort of spinnaker, of which you may see the yard lying along decks in harbour or triced up a little by the halyard, so as to swing clear of the hands.

When the little ships come up like this with either sail well out and square and their course laid straight before the general run of a fresh sea, rolling as they go, it is as though the wind had a friend and companion of its own, understanding all its moods, so easily and rapidly do they arrive towards the shore. A little jib (along this coast at least) is bent along the forestay, and the dark line of it marks the swing and movement of the whole. So also when you stand and look from along their wake and see them leaving for the horizon along a slant of the Levantine, with the breeze just on their quarter and their laden hulls careening a trifle to leeward, you would say they were great birds, born of the sea, and sailing down the current from which they were bred. The peaks of their tall sails have a turn to them like the wing-tips of birds, especially of those darting birds which come up to us from the south after winter and shoot along their way.

Moreover, the sails of these little ships never seem to lose the memory of power. Their curves and fullness always suggest a movement of the hull. Very often at sunset when the dead calm reflects things unbroken like an inland pond, the topmost angle of these lateens catches some hesitating air that stirs above, and leads it down the sail, so that a little ripple trembles round the bows of the boat, though all the water beside them is quite smooth, and you see her gliding in without oars.

44

She comes along in front of the twilight, as gradual and as silent as the evening, and seems to be impelled by nothing more substantial than the advance of darkness.

It is with such companions to proclaim the title of the land that one comes round under a point of hills and enters harbour.

*From " Esto Perpetua "*

# THE SECOND OF NOVEMBER, 1902

I WOKE sharply and suddenly from a dream in that empty room. It was Grizzlebeard that had put his hand upon my shoulder. The late winter dawn was barely glimmering, and there was mist upon the heath outside and rime upon the windows.

I woke and shuddered. For in my dream I had come to a good place, the place inside the mind, which is all made up of remembrance and of peace. Here I had seemed to be in a high glade of beeches, standing on soft, sweet grass on a slope very high above the sea; the air was warm and the sea was answering the sunlight, very far below me. It was such a place as my own Downs have made for me in my mind, but the Downs transfigured, and the place was full of glory and of content, height and great measurement fit for the beatitude of the soul. Nor had I in that dream any memory of loss, but rather a complete end of it, and I was surrounded, though I could not see them, with the return of all those things that had ever been my own. But this was in the dream only; and when I woke it was to the raw world and the sad uncertain beginnings of a little winter day.

Grizzlebeard, who had woken me up, said gravely:

"We must be up early. Let us waken the others also, and take the road, for we are near the end of our journey. We have come to the term and boundary of this short passage of ours, and of our brief companionship, for we must reach the county border in these early hours. So awake, and waken the others."

Then I woke the other two, who also stirred and looked wearily at the thin, grey light, but rose in their turn, and then I said to Grizzlebeard:

46

"Shall we not eat before we start to the place after which we shall not see each other any more?"

But he said, "No, we have but a little way to go, and when we have gone that little way together, we will break a crust between us, and pledge each other if you will, and then we shall never see each other any more."

The others also said that this was the way in which the matter should be accomplished.

Yielding to them, therefore (for I perceived that they were greater than I), we went out into the morning mist and walked through it sturdily enough, but silent, the sounds of our footsteps coming close into our ears, blanketed and curtained by the fog. For a mile and second mile and a third no one of us spoke a word to another. But as I walked along I looked furtively first to one side and then to the other, judging my companions, whom chance had given me for these few hours; and it seemed to me (whether from the mist or what not) that they were taller than men; and their eyes avoided my eyes.

When we had come to Treyford, Grizzlebeard, who was by dumb assent at this moment our leader, or at any rate certainly mine, took that lane northward which turns through Redlands and up to the hill of Elstead and its inn. Then for the first time he spoke and said:

"Here we will break a loaf, and pledge each other for the last time."

Which we did, all sitting quite silent, and then again we took the road, and went forward as we had gone forward before, until we came to Harting. And when we came to Harting, just in the village street of it, Grizzlebeard, going forward a little more quickly, drew with him his two companions, and they stood before me, barring the road as it were, and looking at me kindly, but halting my advance.

47

I said to them, a little afraid, " Do you make for our parting now? We are not yet come to the county border!"

But Grizzlebeard said (the others keeping silent):

" Yes. As we met upon this side of the county border, so shall we part before we cross it. Nor shall you cross it with us. But these my companions and I, when we have crossed it must go each to our own place: but you are perhaps more fortunate, for you are not far from your home."

When he had said this, I was confused to wonder from his voice and from the larger aspect of himself and his companions, whether indeed they were men.

" . . . And is there," I said, " in all the county another such company of four; shall I find even one companion like any of you? Now who is there to-day that can pour out songs as you can at every hour and make up the tunes as well? And even if they could so sing, would any such man or men be of one faith with me?

" Come back with me," I said, " along the crest of the Downs; we will overlook together the groves at Lavington and the steep at Bury Combe, and then we will turn south and reach a house I know of upon the shingle, upon the tide, near where the Roman palaces are drowned beneath the Owers; and to-night once more, and if you will for the last time, by another fire we will sing yet louder songs, and mix them with the noise of the sea."

But Grizzlebeard would not even linger. He looked at me with a dreadful solemnity and said:

" No; we are all three called to other things. But do you go back to your home, for the journey is done."

Then he added (but in another voice): " There is nothing at all that remains: nor any house; nor any

48

castle, however strong; nor any love, however tender and sound; nor any comradeship among men, however hardy. Nothing remains but the things of which I will not speak, because we have spoken enough of them already during these four days. But I who am old will give you advice, which is this—to consider chiefly from now onward those permanent things which are, as it were, the shores of this age and the harbours of our glittering and pleasant but dangerous and wholly changeful sea."

When he had said this (by which he meant Death), the other two, looking sadly at me, stood silent also for about the time in which a man can say good-bye with reverence. Then they all three turned about and went rapidly and with a purpose up the village street.

I watched them, straining my sad eyes, but in a moment the mist received them and they had disappeared

I went up in gloom, by the nearest spur, on to the grass and into the loneliness of the high Downs that are my brothers and my repose; and, once upon their crest, setting my face eastward I walked on in a fever for many hours back towards the places from which we had come; and below me as I went was that good landscape in which I had passed such rare and memorable hours.

I still went on, through little spinnies here and there, and across the great wave tops and rolls of the hills, and as the day proceeded and the light declined about me I still went on, now dipping into the gaps where tracks and roads ran over the chain, now passing for a little space into tall and silent woods wherever these might stand. And all the while I came nearer and nearer to an appointed spot of which a memory had been fixed for years in my mind. But as I strode, with such a goal in view, an increasing loneliness oppressed me, and the

D

49

# HILAIRE BELLOC

air of loss and the echo of those profound thoughts which had filled the last words we four had exchanged together.

It was in the grove above Lavington, near the mounds where they say old kings are buried, that I, still following the crest of my hills, felt the full culmination of all the twenty tides of mutability which had thus run together to make a skerry in my soul. I saw and apprehended, as a man sees or touches a physical thing, that nothing of our sort remains, and that even before my county should cease to be itself I should have left it. I recognized that I was (and I confessed) in that attitude of the mind wherein men admit mortality; something had already passed from me—I mean that fresh and vigorous morning of the eyes wherein the beauty of this land had been reflected as in a tiny mirror of burnished silver. Youth was gone out apart; it was loved and regretted, and therefore no longer possessed.

Then, as I walked through this wood more slowly, pushing before me great billows of dead leaves, as the bows of a ship push the dark water before them, this side and that, when the wind blows full on the middle of the sail and the water answers loudly as the ship sails on, so I went till suddenly I remembered with the pang that catches men at the clang of bells what this time was in November; it was the Day of the Dead. All that day I had so moved and thought alone and fasting, and now the light was falling. I had consumed the day in that deep wandering on the heights alone, and now it was evening. Just at that moment of memory I looked up and saw that I was there. I had come upon that lawn which I had fixed for all these hours to be my goal.

It is the great platform just over Barl'ton, whence all the world lies out before one. Eastward into the night for fifty miles stretched on the wall of the Downs, and it stretched westward towards the coloured sky

50

where a full but transfigured daylight still remained. Southward was the belt of the sea, very broad, as it is from these bare heights, and absolutely still; nor did any animal move in the brushwood near me to insult the majesty of that silence. Northward before me and far below swept the Weald.

The haze had gone; the sky was faint and wintry, but pure throughout its circle, and above the Channel hung largely the round of the moon, still pale, because the dark had not yet come.

But though she had been worshipped so often upon such evenings and from such a place, a greater thing now moved and took me from her, and turning round I looked north from the ridge of the steep escarpment over the plain to the rivers and the roofs of the Weald. I would have blessed them had I known some form of word or spell which might convey an active benediction, but as I knew none such, I repeated instead the list of their names to serve in place of a prayer.

The river Arun, a valley of sacred water; and Amberley Wild brook, which is lonely with reeds at evening; and Burton Great House, where I had spent nights in November; and Lavington also and Hidden Byworth; and Fittleworth next on, and Egdean Side, all heath and air; and the lake and the pine-trees at the mill; and Petworth, little town.

All the land which is knit in with our flesh, and yet in which a man cannot find an acre nor a wall of his own.

I knew as this affection urged me that verse alone would satisfy something at least of that irremediable desire. I lay down therefore at full length upon the short grass which the sheep also love, and taking out a little stump of pencil that I had, and tearing off the back of a letter, I held my words prepared.

HILAIRE BELLOC

My metre, which at first eluded me (though it had been with me in a way for many hours) was given me by these chance lines that came:

> . . . and therefore even youth that dies
> May leave of right its legacies.

I put my pencil upon the paper, doubtfully, and drew little lines, considering my theme. But I would not long hesitate in this manner, for I knew that all creation must be chaos first, and then gestures in the void before it can cast out the completed thing. So I put down in fragments this line and that; and thinking first of how many children below me upon that large and fruitful floor were but entering what I must perforce abandon, I wrote down:

> . . . and of mine opulence I leave
> To every Sussex girl and boy
> My lot in universal joy.

Having written this down, I knew clearly what was in my mind.

The way in which our land and we mix up together and are part of the same thing sustained me, and led on the separate parts of my growing poem towards me; introducing them one by one; till at last I wrote down this further line:

> One with our random fields we grow.

And since I could not for the moment fill in the middle of the verse, I wrote the end, which was already fashioned:

> . . . because of lineage and because
> The soil and memories out of mind
> Embranch and broaden all mankind.

Ah! but if a man is part of and is rooted in one steadfast piece of earth, which has nourished him and given him his being, and if he can on his side lend it glory and

52

do it service (I thought), it will be a friend to him for ever, and he has outflanked Death in a way.

And I shall pass [thought I], but this shall stand
Almost as long as No-Man's Land.

"No, certainly," I answered to myself aloud, "he does not die!" Then from that phrase there ran the fugue, and my last stanzas stood out clear at once, complete and full, and I wrote them down as rapidly as writing can go.

He does not die [I wrote] that can bequeath
Some influence to the land he knows,
Or dares, persistent, interwreath
Love permanent with the wild hedgerows ;
He does not die, but still remains
Substantiate with his darling plains.

The spring's superb adventure calls
His dust athwart the woods to flame ;
His boundary river's secret falls
Perpetuate and repeat his name.
He rides his loud October sky :
He does not die. He does not die.

The beeches know the accustomed head
Which loved them, and a peopled air
Beneath their benediction spread
Comforts the silence everywhere ;
For native ghosts return and these
Perfect the mystery in the trees.

So, therefore, though myself be crosst
The shuddering of that dreadful day
When friend and fire and home are lost
And even children drawn away—
The passer-by shall hear me still,
A boy that sings on Duncton Hill.

Full of these thoughts and greatly relieved by their metrical expression, I went, through the gathering darkness, southward across the Downs to my home.

*From " The Four Men "*

53

# LONDON RIVER

THROUGH the flats that bound the North Sea and shelve into it imperceptibly, merging at last with the shallow flood, and re-emerging in distant sandbanks and less conspicuous shoals, run facing each other two waterways far inland, which are funnels and entries, as it were, scoured by the tide.

Each has at the end of the tideway a narrow, placid, inland stream, from whence the broader, noisier sea part also takes its name. Each has been and will always be famous in the arms and in the commerce of Europe. Each forms a sort of long great street of ships crowded in a traffic to and fro. For each has its great port. The one Antwerp, the other London. The Scheldt is the name of the first, which leads to Antwerp, and makes the opportunity for that great market of the world. But the second is the River of London, much older in its destinies, and probably more destined to endure in its functions of commerce.

I know not how to convey that picture in the mind, which the eyes do not see, and yet by which a man is haunted if he has read enough of books and seen the maps, when he comes up through the Narrows of Dover Straits from the wide, empty seas three days behind and knows that there lies before his owner a choice between the eastern and the western gate. That choice is in the case of every ship determined long before. She has the dull duty to do of turning to the right or to the left, and her orders bind her to the river of the Netherlands or of England as it may be. But if you will consider many centuries and the changing adventures of business you

54

will still—as you pass northward between the two shores of Flanders and of Britain, and as you see their recession upon either side of the northern way which opens before you—understand that doubt upon the future and the rivalry of the two rivers which is soon to be so deeply impressed upon the politics of our time.

I could think of the Scheldt and of the Thames as two antagonists facing each other before conflict across a marked arena, which is that of the shallow, tumbling, and yellow water of the North Sea; or as two forces pitted one against the other, streams each of which would force the other back if it could find the strength; or as two Courts in a perpetual jealousy one of the other, intriguing and making and losing point after point in a game of polity.

When the statisticians have done their talk—and very brainless it is—of resources and of metals, two opposing *lives* are left standing behind either of the great towns, and either of the great sea rivers. The one is the experiment of the modern Germanies; the other is the founded tradition of England; and the more closely a man considers each of these the greater contrast does he discover between the causes of either's energy of come and go.

A third great tidal river is also concerned with these seas, also helps to determine their commerce, also supports its great inland town. That river is the Seine, and I shall, in the pages which follow, use the Seine also for the example it affords in the analogies and contrasts and parallels which I propose to draw. But it is the Scheldt and the Thames which still remain the greater opponents. The united political life of Gaul, which was inherited and transformed by the French Monarchy forbade the growth of a great commerce to the north. Paris became not only the political centre of France but its main market as well, and to-day the water carriage of Paris—that is, the traffic of its port—is greater than that of any maritime town in the country. Only if Normandy had developed as an independent state would Rouen have become what Antwerp and London have become. Rouen would then have been, without doubt, the point of transhipment between the inland and the maritime waterways, and the distance of the town from coal would hardly have affected it more than does the distance of London. Its situation as a political junction would have determined its greatness. As it is the Lower Seine may be set beside the Scheldt and the Thames for an illustration in their topography and in the origins of their human settlements, but it does not afford a true commercial parallel to-day, and Rouen is no third rival to the two great ports which are before our eyes and in this generation struggling for primacy.

It is the custom of sailors to speak of that water by which they approach a great town under the name of the town. Men coming up from Yarmouth Roads inland do not speak of the Yare, but of Norwich River. For to the sailor the river is but a continuation of, or an access to, his port, and the Lower Thames is thus universally known from the sea as London River. The term is an accidental one, but it contains the true history of the connexion between the stream and the town. The Thames made London. London is a function of the Thames, and it is in such a connexion that I propose to regard it in this essay: London as the great crossing place of the Thames, and as the custodian and fruit of what early may have been the chief ferry, but has for nearly two thousand years been the chief bridge; London as the market of which the Thames is the approach and the port; London as a habitation of which the great street is the Thames, a street for centuries the main highway of its people, lost for a time and now recovering its ancient use; London as the civil and religious head of revenues which were drawn from the Thames Valley; and London as the determinant, through its position upon the Thames, of English military history.

This intimate connexion between the city and the river we all instinctively feel, and the two are connected together as no other waterway with its capital can be connected throughout Europe. For the Thames is all that every other river is to every other capital wherever some great stream is connected with a chief city. But whereas in every other case it is but one or another of the functions of such a stream that history can remark, in the case of London it can remark them all. Little sea-borne traffic reaches Paris by the Seine; the Tiber could never be a street for Rome; Vienna neglects the Danube; Antwerp protects no great crossing, nor has ever been the nucleus of a State; Rouen—the nearest parallel—was not the strategical pivot of Normandy, nor ever formed, as London forms, a chief fraction in the economic power of its province. The two rivers which are sacred to Lyons never fed that town; the Rhone watered but did not lead to Arles. The towns of Lombardy depend upon the fertility of the Po Valley, but the stream is nothing to their commerce or to their political eminence, and Milan, and Venice, and Turin are independent of it. Saragossa was the mistress of Arragon, but the Ebro did not make Saragossa, and as for Madrid, the trickle which runs below Madrid is best described in the story of the Spanish patriot who was dying of thirst after battle, but upon being offered a cup of water, said, "Give it to the poor Manzanares." Lisbon and Cadiz are maritime, not fluvial, and look where you will throughout the civilization of Europe you will not find, save in the case of London, this complete interdependence between a great town and its river.

In tracing or establishing this intimate bond between London and the Thames one must guard against an error which the modern reader rightly suspects and is justly ready to criticize or to deny when it appears in any piece of historical writing. That error is the error of materialism.

A generation ago it was universal, and there was no phenomenon in the story of England or of Europe from the emplacement of a city to the growth of the Church which was not traced to inanimate causes superior to, and independent of, any action of the Will. This philosophy narrowed, distorted, and dried up every department of knowledge, and while the area or learning increased with a rapidity hitherto unknown, the spirit inhabiting that conquest was starved. It was as though the time could not contain at once the energy to discover and the energy to know, and as though the covering of so vast a field in so short a period was achieved inevitably at a cost of profundity. That a bias towards the mechanical and the necessary should be present in the physical sciences—in chemistry for instance—is to be expected, that it should have invaded biology was less excusable, but that it should have been permitted to affect (as it did) the business native to man —his building, his institutions, his very dreams—was an excessive blunder, and the spirit of all the younger men to-day is running if anything too strongly in reaction against that ebb-tide of the soul. They reject the dogmas of their fathers which would bend everything man has done to material circumstance, which would talk of man as the slave rather than the master of

58

his instruments, and which, in an argument absurdly circular, "interpreted history in the terms of Economics": and they are right.

Even in the sphere of topography, where the physical limitations of human action are the main subject of the writer, they expect a full admission of the soul of man and even—which is very wise—some recognition of that mysterious genius which inhabits every place and is perhaps its vital part.

They are right. No one can see the marriage between London and its river without wondering in what degree things other than ponderable and measurable things may enter into the habitation of man. There is nothing man does, of course, which has not in it the soul. But it may be also true that there is nothing done to man wherein some soul is not also. Now the homes of man and the air and the water and the wind and the earth, against which in part and with which in part those homes arise, are so woven in with his fate—which is a spiritual fate—that we must properly lend to these insensate things some controlling motive; and we may rightly say, though only by the use of metaphor, that all these things have a spirit within them. I cannot get away from it that the Thames may be alive, and London most certainly is.

But all these things, though one may put them in the form of statements, are really questions; and questions to which no sort of answer has yet been discovered.

*From " The River of London "*

# BIBLIOGRAPHY

*(The publishers of books at present out of print are not given.)*

1895 : *Verses and Sonnets* (Duckworth).

1896 : *The Bad Child's Book of Beasts* (Duckworth).

1897 : *More Beasts for Worse Children* (Duckworth).

1898 : *The Modern Traveller.*

1899 : *Danton* (Methuen).  *Moral Alphabet.*

1900 : *Paris* (Methuen).  *Lambkin's Remains* (Duckworth).

1901 : *Robespierre.*

1902 : *The Path to Rome* (Allen and Unwin; cheap edition, Nelson).

1903 : *Caliban's Guide to Letters* (Duckworth).

1904 : *The Old Road* (Constable).  *Avril* (Duckworth). *Emmanuel Burden* (Methuen).

1906 : *Hills and the Sea* (Methuen).  *Esto Perpetua* (Duckworth).

1907 : *The Historic Thames* (Dent).

1908 : *Mr Clutterbuck's Election* (Eveleigh Nash).  *The Eyewitness. On Nothing* (Methuen).

1909 : *Marie Antoinette* (Methuen).  *The Pyrenees* (Methuen).  *On Everything* (Methuen).  *A Change in the Cabinet. Cautionary Tales* (Duckworth).

1910 : *Pongo and the Bull* (Long).  *On Something* (Methuen). *On Anything* (Methuen).

1911 : *The Girondin. Warfare in England* (Williams and Norgate).  *The French Revolution* (Williams and Norgate).  *First and Last* (Methuen). *British Battle Books* (Rees).

# HILAIRE BELLOC

1912 : *The Servile State. The Green Overcoat* (Arrowsmith)
*This, That, and the Other* (Methuen). *The Four Men* (Nelson).

1913 : *The Stane Street* (Constable). *The River of London.*

1914 : *The Book of the Bayeux Tapestry.*

1915–16 : *A General Sketch of the European War.*

1916 : *The Last Days of the French Monarchy.*

1918 : *The Free Press* (Allen and Unwin).

1920 : *The House of Commons and Monarchy* (Allen and Unwin). *Europe and the Faith* (Constable).

1922 : *The Jews* (Constable). *The Mercy of Allah* (Chatto and Windus).

1923 : *On* (Methuen). *The Contrast* (Arrowsmith).

1924 : *The Road* (Fisher Unwin). *The Campaign of* 1812 *and the Retreat from Moscow* (Nelson). *Economics for Helen* (Arrowsmith).

1925 : *Mr Petre, a Novel* (Arrowsmith). *A History of England* (Methuen). *The Cruise of the " Nona "* (Constable).